Dedicated to La Brea Tar Pits scientists Dr. Emily Lindsey, paleoecologist, and Dr. Reagan Dunn, paleobotanist. —J. U.

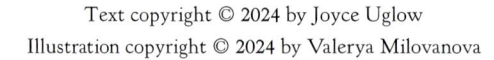

Text copyright © 2024 by Joyce Uglow
Illustration copyright © 2024 by Valerya Milovanova

Bushel & Peck Books is a family-run publishing house based in Fresno, California, that
believes in uplifting children with the highest standards of art, music, literature, and ideas.
Find beautiful books for gifted young minds at www.bushelandpeckbooks.com.

Our family is dedicated to fighting illiteracy all over the world. For every book we sell, we
donate one to a child in need—book for book. To nominate a school or an organization
to receive free books, please visit www.bushelandpeckbooks.com.

Type set in Calder and LTC Kennerley.
Endpaper pattern licensed from Shutterstock.com

LCCN: 2024941068
ISBN: 978-1-63819-188-9

First Edition

Printed in China

1 3 5 7 9 10 8 6 4 2

Stuck!

The Story of La Brea Tar Pits

JOYCE UGLOW

ILLUSTRATED BY

VALERYA MILOVANOVA

BUSHEL
& PECK
BOOKS

Thousands of years ago,
unsuspecting ice age animals
were drawn to shallow water . . .

only to find oozing, oily stickiness.

Harlan's Ground Sloth lumbered,
meandering, making a meal
of wheatgrass and willow,
wanting a cool drink.

She slowed.

Struggled.

Unable to move on.

Stuck!

Smilodon bared a sharp-saber smile.
Then sniffed, stalked . . .
pounced on Sloth.

Stuck!

Trapped!

No need to
pin down prey
already captured.

Dire wolves followed the scents and groans.
They entered the fray of predator-prey—
but instead of a meal,
a sticky feel.

Errant Eagle landed,
ripping into the mess.
No get-and-go supper—
just mysterious muck.

Stuck!

Trapped!

Sunk!

Stacked!

Vultures ventured in for some scraps.
La Brea Condor, too.
Flies, wasps, dragonflies, and beetles followed.
An entire ecosystem jumbled together,
unlucky predators and prey in stacks.

Storks, vultures, condors,
cedars, redwoods, cottonwoods,
rainbow trout from local streams,
blue-eyed grasses, knotweed,
tadpoles, turtles, snakes, snails,
seeds, cones, pollen, leaves,
the oldest of the old at the bottom . . .

Unnoticed.

Menageries trapped together
under seeping asphalt and sediment.

Unknown.

Tiny fossil treasures
mingled with
American lions and short-faced bears,
saturated and preserved.

Underground.

In summertime's warmth,
asphalt pools bubbled,
softening,
trapping more.

Even giants.

Covered by time and sediment
that washed over the basin.

Weighed down.

Broken.

Jumbled.

Knotted.

Waiting . . .

waiting . . .

waiting . . .

waiting . . .

Until
oil field workers
found much more than oil!

Unearthed!

Uncovered!

Scientists brush bits into buckets,
sorting stories
grain by grain.

The Tar Pits time capsule tells millions of stories.
Layered clues about the past reveal the secrets of our planet.

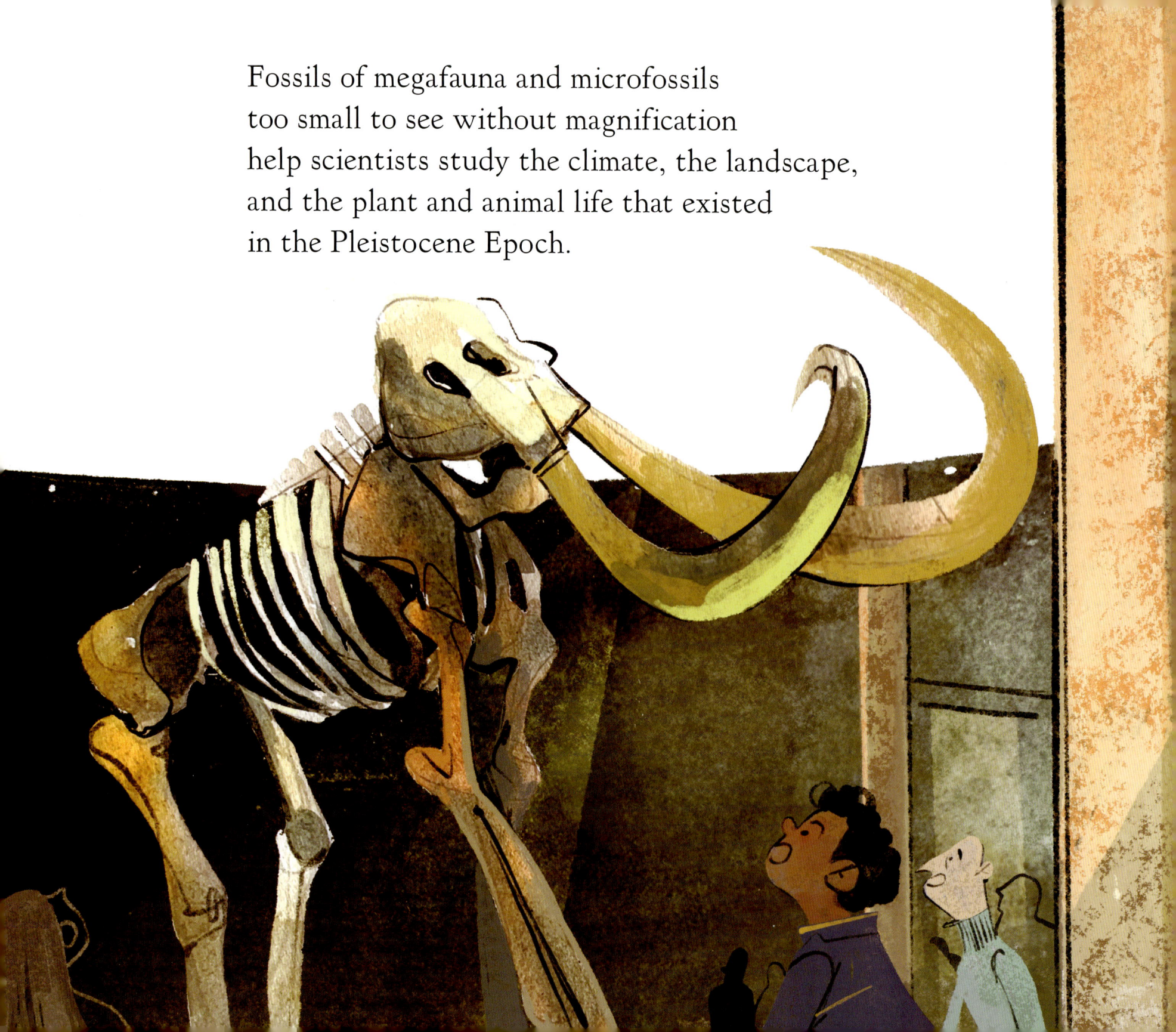

Fossils of megafauna and microfossils
too small to see without magnification
help scientists study the climate, the landscape,
and the plant and animal life that existed
in the Pleistocene Epoch.

Scientists discover, prepare, research,
and display it all in one place.
They piece the past together,
imagining the future.

This is not
the end of
the story.

Surrounded by traffic, skyscrapers, and movie stars,
Dragonfly searches the sunny skies of Los Angeles,
zigzags across a parking lot,

soars sideways,

darts up,

looking for a place
to lay her eggs.

dipping down,

She slows, looks . . .

and flies on,
to find a pond . . .

without bubbles.

La Brea Tar Pits Time Capsule

$\int$cientists report that oil below Los Angeles formed millions of years after the dinosaurs went extinct. Then, 100,000 years ago, the ocean receded to reveal land, and 50,000 years ago, Earth's cracks allowed oil to seep upward onto the land. At that time, much of North America was covered in miles of ice. Ice age animals roamed the land looking for habitats and food that fit their needs. Some of those animals stumbled into stickiness and became stranded. For example, 27 mammoths got mired in the muck of Pit 9, but that did not happen in one day or even one year. It took thousands of years to entrap that many mammoths in one place. Pit 91 has active seeping to this day. How many more days, years, decades, or even centuries do you think this pattern will continue?

CHANGES!	SEEPS!	STUCK!	PURCHASED!	DIGS!	THIS IS NOT THE END OF THE STORY.
5 TO 25 MILLION YEARS AGO	**2.5 MILLION TO 11,700 YEARS AGO**	**50,000 TO 10,000 YEARS AGO**	**19TH CENTURY**	**20TH CENTURY**	**21ST CENTURY**
During the Miocene Epoch, oil formed from marine plankton that died and dropped to the ocean basin floor. Over time, pressure and heat converted the organisms into oil. A reservoir formed.	The end of the last ice age happened during the Pleistocene Epoch. Cracks in the Earth's crust allowed oil to seep to the surface 50,000 years ago. Stickiness pooled on land, hidden.	An ice age ecosystem got stuck and stacked in the mysterious stickiness. The climate and environment changed over time. A great many animals went extinct.	Ida and Henry Hancock farmed the 4,439-acre Rancho La Brea in the 1880s. The Hancocks mined for oil on the land. They found unusual bones.	In 1907, high school students helped scientists dig up the bones. Between 1913 and 1915, volunteers and scientists dug up thousands of fossils from 96 deposits. More than 100 deposits have been found.	Scientists learn from the 3.5 million fossils of animal bones, seeds, twigs, snake bones, fish teeth, and dung beetles. They help us learn about climate changes and much more for our future.

Glossary

ASPHALT: A sticky, black substance found at La Brea Tar Pits. Also known as asphaltum, bitumen, or pitch (*brea* in Spanish), it seeps up from the Salt Lake Oil Field below. Prehistoric animals and plants became trapped in the asphalt, leading to their preservation as fossils.

CLIMATE CHANGE: Shifts in weather patterns over long periods. Dr. Regan Dunn's research at La Brea shows how a past warming period and increased dryness changed the ecosystem, impacting plants and animals, with some adapting and others becoming extinct.

ECOSYSTEM: A community of living and nonliving things interacting with each other. It includes weather, plants, animals, and other organisms. La Brea's ecosystem changed over time, influencing which species thrived or struggled.

ENTRAPMENT EVENTS: Instances when animals became stuck in the asphalt. This occurred sporadically, often when animals sought water, migrated, or hunted. The asphalt pools were hidden by water, dust, or leaves, and their stickiness varied with temperature.

EXTINCT: Species that no longer exist anywhere on Earth. Extinction can result from environmental changes, habitat loss, natural disasters, or evolutionary processes. La Brea's fossils reveal many extinct species, offering insights into past life.

EXTANT: Species that still exist today. Some prehistoric species found at La Brea, like pronghorns and certain bees, have survived to modern times, highlighting the continuity of life alongside extinction.

FOSSIL: Evidence of ancient life, typically over 10,000 years old. At La Brea, fossils include bones, teeth, plants, and even insects, preserved in the asphalt and providing a window into the past.

MEGAFAUNA: Large animals weighing over 100 pounds. La Brea is famous for its megafauna fossils, including mammoths, saber-toothed cats, and giant sloths, showcasing the impressive diversity of past life.

MICROFOSSIL: Tiny fossils visible only with magnification. These include pollen, seeds, and small insects, revealing details about the ancient environment and food webs at La Brea.

PALEONTOLOGIST: A scientist who studies ancient life through fossils. Paleontologists at La Brea carefully excavate and analyze fossils, piecing together the story of this unique prehistoric site.

PITS: Cone-shaped deposits formed by layers of asphalt, animal remains, and sediment accumulating over time. These pits are the source of La Brea's remarkable fossil collection.

PLEISTOCENE: The geological epoch spanning from 2.5 million to 11,700 years ago, characterized by a series of ice ages. While Los Angeles wasn't covered in ice, the climate fluctuations during the Pleistocene impacted La Brea's ecosystem.

SEEP: A place where oil or asphalt naturally oozes to the surface. At La Brea, seeps formed shallow pools, attracting animals and leading to their entrapment and eventual fossilization.

SEDIMENT: Material like sand, mud, and pebbles that is transported and deposited by wind or water. Sediment layers at La Brea buried trapped animals and plants, contributing to their preservation as fossils.

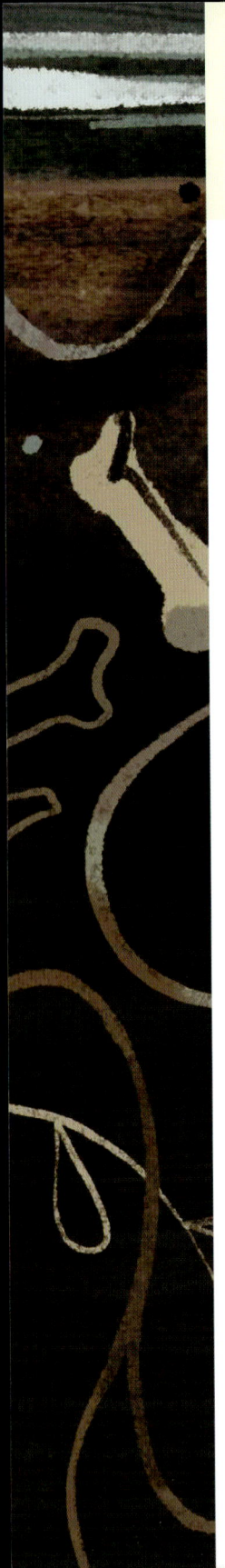

Who's Trapped?

- Agile kangaroo rat
- American badger
- American lion
- American mastodon
- Antique bison
- Arboreal salamander
- Arizona toad
- Black-tailed jackrabbit
- Bobcat
- Black racer snake
- Carp
- Clam
- Cougar
- Coyote
- Columbian mammoth
- Coot
- Conifer
- Crane
- Cricket
- Common side-blotched lizard
- Damselfly
- Dragonfly
- Desert spiny lizard
- Dire wolf
- Dove
- Dusky-footed woodrat
- Dwarf pronghorn
- Errant eagle

- Earwig
- Falcon
- Fragile eagle
- Frog
- Goose
- Giant jaguar
- Glossy snake
- Gray fox
- Grizzly bear
- Ground sloth
- Gull
- Harlan's ground sloth
- Hawk
- Heron
- Hoary bat
- Ibis
- Iguana
- Juniper
- Kangaroo rat
- Large-headed llama
- Long-nosed snake
- Lungless salamander
- Locust
- Long-horned bison
- Merriam's chipmunk
- Mastodon
- Millipede
- Monterey cypress
- Nightjar

- New world antelope
- Nuttall's scrub
- Owl
- Peccary
- Pelican
- Pigeon
- Pit viper
- Plover
- Puma
- Pocket mouse
- Poorwill
- Quail
- Raccoon
- Rail
- Red deer
- Ringtail
- Roadrunner
- Saber-toothed cat
- Salmon
- Scorpion
- Sedge
- Short-faced bear
- Shrew
- Skink
- Songbird
- Spider
- Spotted skunk
- Stickleback
- Stork

- Tapir
- Teratorn
- Tick
- Treehopper
- Trout
- Turkey
- Turtle
- Vole
- Vulture
- Water flea
- Weasel
- Western horse
- Willow
- Whiptail lizard
- Woodpecker
- Yesterday's camel

| AMPHIBIAN |
| BIRD |
| MAMMAL |
| FISH |
| REPTILE |
| INVERTEBRATE |
| PLANT |

More About La Brea Tar Pits

Today, skyscrapers in Los Angeles stand near Hancock Park where fenced-off asphalt bubbles up through the pavement in its parking lot! Unfortunately, unsuspecting insects, birds, squirrels, and lizards still get stuck in the mysterious stickiness.

Since the early 1900s, when George Hancock's oil field workers noticed something unusual, millions of fossils have been pulled up from the asphalt deposits, cleaned, sorted, pieced together, studied, and displayed.

But millions more fossils may be found when the unopened crates from Project 23 get examined. In 2006, construction at the Los Angeles County Museum of Art (LACMA) parking garage halted when they discovered "Zed," a Columbian mammoth, "parked" underground.

Unlike other fossils found at La Brea, Zed didn't get mired in muck. Scientists believe that Zed died and was swept away by a nearby stream, and *then* got covered in asphalt. Zed, along with fish and snails of the time, were preserved together. Project 23 is named for the 23 boxes of asphalt deposits unearthed and removed from the construction site at LACMA.

La Brea Tar Pits are an unparalleled living laboratory. They're officially known as one of the first 100 Geological Heritage Sites in the world—special places where Earth's history is preserved. The Tar Pits are the only active urban excavation site with more ice age fossils than any other location. The millions of fossils discovered reveal more than 600 different ice age species of plants and animals.

At the time that Pit 4 was active (24,000 to 14,000 years ago), half of North America was covered by ice sheets. By comparison, when Pits 61 to 67 were active (less than 10,000 years ago) the climate around La Brea Tar Pits was similar to what California experiences today. Fossil records show stories of the changes in the animals' body sizes and that their diets evolved over time. But as the ice retreated and the temperatures got warmer, lakes and streams dried up. Some animals couldn't adapt to the new weather or changes in the food supply. Most of the La Brea megafauna went extinct 14,000 to 11,000 years ago.

Fossils fill our hearts with wonder and show us changes over time, even revealing that Los Angeles was once covered by an ocean! Scientists find climate science stories within fossils, noticing how changes forced animals and plants to evolve. Research on preserved remains, such as a fossilized beetle's wing and the food that got stuck in an ancient camel's teeth, tell how plants and animals changed.

FOSSILS INSPIRE US TO THINK ABOUT OUR FUTURE

- What can we do to be sure our actions don't harm the environment?
- What mysteries will you unearth and unlock in your future?
- Will your job someday be one where you dig in to understand life on Earth?

About the Author

JOYCE P. UGLOW has been asking questions and collecting words since an early age. Retired, she now writes picture books and poetry for children who are also intrigued by words and our wondrous world—books that educators, librarians, and kids tell each other about. She currently serves as SCBWI Wisconsin's Assistant Regional Advisor and is on the Board of the Wisconsin Center for the Book. She digs in on topics from whales, rocks, bees, trees, and families to ancient cave art and fossils trapped in asphalt seeps and everything in between, and she is unwaveringly committed to sparking kids' interests.

About the Illustrator

VALERYA MILOVANOVA is an illustrator and artist based in Hatfield, UK. Valerya moved to the UK for University, graduating from the University of Hertfordshire in illustration and graphic design. She is a proud participant of the MOTS Illustration Festival 2023 and her children's picture book, *I Am Upset*, was shortlisted for the Batsford Prize.

BUSHEL & PECK BOOKS

About the Publisher

BUSHEL & PECK BOOKS is a children's publishing house with a special mission. Through our Book-for-Book Promise™, we donate one book to kids in need for every book we sell. Our beautiful books are given to kids through schools, libraries, local neighborhoods, shelters, nonprofits, and also to many selfless organizations that are working hard to make a difference. So thank you for purchasing this book! Because of you, another book will find its way into the hands of a child who needs it most.

TO NOMINATE AN ORGANIZATION TO RECEIVE FREE BOOKS, PLEASE VISIT BUSHELANDPECKBOOKS.COM.